HEREFORDSHIRE PEOPLE

BRITAIN

IN OLD PHOTOGRAPHS

HEREFORDSHIRE PEOPLE

LAURENCE MEREDITH

SUTTON PUBLISHING

Sutton Publishing Limited
Phoenix Mill · Thrupp · Stroud
Gloucestershire · GL5 2BU

First published 2003

Copyright © Laurence Meredith, 2003

Title page photograph: Farm workers drinking cider from a traditional cask encased in a wicker basket.

British Library Cataloguing in Publication Data
A catalogue record for this book is available from the British Library.

ISBN 0-7509-2996-0

Typeset in 10.5/13.5 Photina.
Typesetting and origination by Sutton Publishing Limited.
Printed and bound in England by J.H. Haynes & Co. Ltd, Sparkford.

Chaos reigns supreme on Britain's beleaguered rail network but, thanks to local steam enthusiasts, many old engines are kept running in first rate order. Volunteers give freely of their time to keep their hobby alive.

CONTENTS

It's interesting to reflect on prominent advertising in this Bromyard shop window at the beginning of the twentieth century. Oxo and Woodbines have survived, while Wills Gold Flake hasn't. The traditional style of baby pram made something of a comeback in the 1990s, but the clothing worn by the three people – of Victorian origins – has gone presumably for ever.

INTRODUCTION

The presenter of a television holiday programme recently made himself unpopular by describing Herefordshire as having little or nothing in the way of attractions for tourists. There are many people I know, both residents and visitors, who frequently describe the county as 'sleepy' – a place where little happens – a dullard's paradise – an anorak's retreat – and on the face of it they might be right. There is, however, an abundance of evidence to prove that they are wrong.

In the past ten years or so the population of the shire has expanded rapidly; new buildings – housing in particular – have been constructed on land once used for agriculture, and people from all over Britain and some parts of mainland Europe – charmed by the quiet, and largely bucolic nature of the county – have moved in.

As a Herefordshire resident, both townie and countryman, for more than forty years, I have studied the changing nature of the place with a largely sociological interest. Despite the Internet and other inventions of the modern world, which open up the possibility of new horizons and goals for everyone, Herefordshire folk remain largely cautious, restrained and conservative. Social stratification is still well defined, particularly in country areas, and the influence of Welsh culture, built many centuries ago, is almost, but not quite, as tangible as ever.

As a boy much of my summer break from school involved helping Gramps with the harvest on his farm. A Massey Ferguson towed a binder around the fields for several weeks, and we prayed that bad weather wouldn't bring proceedings to a halt. Today, farmers continue to curse the weather, of course, but families can no longer be seen out in the fields at any time of year. Modern machinery – vast, powerful tractors, combine harvesters and ingenious implements – dispense with most tasks, including the traditional harvest, in a matter of hours.

The great cultural 'institutions' will, however, be with us for ever. Afternoon tea, fights among drunks after the pubs have closed, homemade pickles, chutneys and jam, village cricket, the Three Choirs Festival, beef, cider, Hereford United FC and suspicion of anything new have characterised Herefordshire and its folks for many years.

Like a significant number of people in the majority of British counties, many Herefordshire folk speak in the local brogue, which varies from area to area. The 'satellite' towns of Kington, Bromyard, Ross-on-Wye, Ledbury, Leominster and surrounding villages all have their own distinctive lilt, while many living within the boundaries of the city hold a 'dialect' of their own. In many cases it's possible to pinpoint the exact location of a person's upbringing by the way in which he or she speaks. Swearing, and expressing politically incorrect opinions on all subjects, is, and always has been, part and parcel of being Herefordian, irrespective of social background.

Members of Hereford Rowing Club, 1891. From left to right they are: J. Gibbon, T.W. Meats, F.W. Dutton, H.J. Hammonds and W. Mereweather, winners of the Tradesman's Plate, Bewdley Regatta.

Once a great shaper of opinion and behaviour, the influence of the established Church has declined to the point where its 'wares' are viewed as insignificant and irrelevant. Hereford United's meteoric rise from the Southern League to the Second Division in the 1970s compared with the club's current obscurity and financial crisis also illustrates changing social opinion. Whereas the Edgar Street terraces were once packed with enthusiastic fans, the same people now visit PC World on a Saturday afternoon.

By contrast Hereford has a thriving theatre. Twenty-five years ago it hadn't a theatre at all, for this branch of culture was not high on the agenda of the predominantly working-class population. In some respects, traditional values have been eroded and replaced, while the standard of education in the county's schools has, despite anecdotal and unfounded opinion to the contrary in some quarters, risen inexorably.

Although globally famous for cider – H.P. Bulmer is the world's largest manufacturer – Hereford cattle and the Credenhill-based Special Air Service, the county proudly boasts of several well-known celebrities with local connections. Everyone knows of Nell Gwynne, Roger Kemble and David Garrick, but in more recent times the Revd Francis Kilvert, who lived near Clyro and was buried at Bredwardine church, achieved a degree of posterity for his diary, which became widely read during the 1970s and was serialised on television a decade later. Today, the ex-chairman of ICI, Sir John Harvey-Jones, also lives near Clyro.

During the nineteenth century Alfred Watkins invented a form of photographic light meter and formulated his theory of ley lines in Herefordshire. French research during the 1970s indicates that Watkins's ley-line theory is (arguably) correct. At roughly the same

Hereford United Reserves, Birmingham League, 1947/8 season. Back row, left to right: Clunie, Lovett, Glover, Bradley (trainer). Middle row: Gallagher, Lowe, Robertson, McGuire, Morton. Front row: Arlington, Marshall, Bruce.

time the painter Brian Hatton was making a name for himself, while the county's most famous artist today, Peter Manders, continues to work for local publications, despite huge success with his work around the world.

One-time Hereford resident Sir Edward Elgar was as famous locally for his love of cycling as he was internationally for his ability to compose classical music.

Oxford don and children's writer C.S. Lewis was a visitor to the Golden Valley, and actress Miranda Richardson, who played the part of Queenie in the television comedy *Blackadder*, is also a frequent visitor to this same part of rural Herefordshire. Famous footballers John Charles and Tom Best both played for the local team, while Herefordshire's Kevin Sheedy achieved success with Everton during the 1980s.

Politically, Herefordshire folk are liberal conservatives – ordinary, everyday people punctuated by the usual crop of characters, fools, rogues (lovable and otherwise) and strays. It's many years since anyone was hanged in the City – the old gaol where capital punishment was practised was on the site of today's principal bus station in Commercial Road – but serious crime is still not unknown. A number of old boys I've listened to down many years continue to express the view that hanging should be reintroduced for all crimes committed by people under the age of twenty-five, but thankfully our political masters in Westminster have failed to act on their advice.

Every week since eighteen-hundred-and-frozen-to-death the *Hereford Times* has published reports about theft from farms, pub brawls, violent disputes between lovers, purges on cyclists who ride at night without lights, and corpses discovered floating in the River Wye. The newspaper's archive makes it quite clear that human nature, in Herefordshire at least, has not changed in centuries.

While the great Victorian mental hospital, St Mary's at Burghill (known locally as the Nonsense Palace), once catered for up to 600 patients, the city's modern Stonebow Unit has just fifty-four beds, despite a massive increase in population since the 1970s. Debate over the National Health Service plays a large role in local politics, as elsewhere in the country, but in recent times it has become apparent that the most pressing political issue is that of traffic congestion. Hereford is just about the only city in Europe (Dublin is another) that has a relief road running right through its centre. Everyone agrees that a bypass is needed, but agreement as to its route is impossible, which is why a new relief road will never be built. That's how things are in this particular shire.

In the late 1990s the city literally started to go backwards, after a decision by the council to reverse the direction of traffic flowing through certain parts of Hereford. Few motorists agreed with the council that this was a good idea. As an experiment it was an interesting disaster and after indignant and vociferous outcry from locals who failed to understand the fun to be had from acting upon the instructions of contradictory signposts, the system was returned, more or less, to normal.

Naturally, the county is well served by restaurants, the cuisine of many nationalities being represented – Hereford even has a 'drive-in' branch of McDonald's – and every conceivable sports facility is abundantly available, but one tenet of human nature that is certainly not entertained, or tolerated, is sex. One small sex shop in Hereford's Widemarsh Street closed; planning permission for another was not granted. A photographic exhibition at the city library in 2001 – to have included a section devoted to naked people – went ahead but without the nudes! Ironically, pornography can be freely purchased from the top shelves of many newsagents.

Thirty years ago Hereford was without a traditional nightclub. Those seeking evening entertainment attended the Park Hall Ballroom at Wormelow, while live bands regularly appeared at the now defunct Redhill venue. Today the city has a number of extremely successful nightclubs, frequented by people of all ages who enjoy dancing to a brand of noise pollution of which any aeroplane engine manufacturer would be proud.

Like all other areas of Britain, the county has, and copes with, a wide variety of social problems ranging from homelessness to drug-taking. Police, social services, Alcoholics Anonymous and the Samaritans all serve to remind the community of human frailty. Interestingly, a Hereford policeman, who'd spent much of his adult life working in the local drug squad, admitted as he lay dying of lung cancer that morphine (prescribed by a doctor) was of the greatest comfort.

For all their caution, suspicion, problems and the sheer stress of modern living, Herefordians have made progress in so many ways. Four hundred years ago the average adult life expectancy of thirty-nine was largely the result of poor housing and disease. Poor housing still exists but many life-threatening diseases have, of course, been eradicated.

While serious conflict between nations continues, as ever, to threaten world peace and stability – SAS helicopter movements over the city serve as a constant reminder that human beings can't always get on with each other – the folk of Herefordshire carry on business as normal: working, shopping, driving, pubbing, clubbing, cursing, sweating, eating and sleeping just as they always have.

Laurence Meredith

Ancient sculptures on many county churches – this one at Docklow – have survived the ravages of weather surprisingly well. This fellow doesn't appear to have much to smile about.

1

From Cave to Cathedral

Images similar to this are to be found widely in Herefordshire churches. They provide evidence of a society centuries ago that, in part at least, leaned towards culture and civilisation.

Herefordshire probably didn't become a county with well-defined borders until the seventh century, but there is evidence of continuous human habitation in this part of the country over 130,000 years. Paleolithic hunters are known to have occupied King Arthur's Cave near Monmouth in this pre-historic age, and a small number of stone weapons and other artefacts from the site are preserved.

In more recent times – roughly 4,000 years ago – a communal burial chamber was erected above the village of Dorstone. Known as Arthur's Stone, but commonly referred to in reference books as Thor's Stone, Thor-stein or Thor's altar, this ancient monument still stands today, even though weathering has substantially reduced its once impressive dimensions. Its connection with the mythical King Arthur, however, is tenuous.

Some believe that King Arthur, whose reign is not reliably recorded, operated in parts of Herefordshire. Much of Arthurian lore emanates, of course, from Sir Thomas Malory's *Morte d'Arthur*, written between 1460 and 1468, in which the central figure is portrayed as a great hero. On the other hand, Welsh scripts of the eighth and ninth centuries also make reference to Arthur, but describe him more in the nature of a cattle rustler – a border raider without scruples.

In her book *Arthurian Links with Herefordshire* Mary Andere gives an account of a woman who, after stopping her car and looking across the Wye Valley near Hoarwithy, claims that she saw Arthur and ten or so of his men in a 'vision'. Such phenomena are not uncommon but largely serve to underline that myths and visions make for interesting bedfellows, and 'bar babble' after closing time.

The Romans left an abundance of evidence of their habitation of the county, but recorded very little about their stay. Cynics have suggested that this was because they, like visitors today, found little to excite them, with the possible exception of an occasional exchange of abuse with marauding Celts. They finally left Britain altogether early in the fifth century.

Two hundred years later the Church was established; *monasteria* (minsters) housing religious communities became part and parcel of the cultural and institutional landscape. Such was the Church's influence and wealth that its power wouldn't wane and dissipate until 1945 and, arguably, beyond. Naturally, the Church guarded its power jealously in the name of God, and 'regional' kings did much the same.

There was, however, great rivalry between kings. In 794, for example, King Offa ordered Aethelbert's head to be struck off. His body was thrown into a marsh near the River Lugg, but was rescued by Offa's chamberlain, Berthtferth, who was told in a vision to raise the body and take it in an ox cart to Fernlage near the River Wye. As Berthferth was approaching the village of Lyde, Aethelbert's head rolled off the cart. It was discovered by a blind man who stumbled across it. This, seemingly, resulted in the man recovering his sight and, with his macabre prize, he ran after the cart so that the head could be reunited with the body. Later the corpse was buried and venerated by King Milferth, who built a a minster over the grave. At this time the place formerly known as

Robert de Lotharingian, bishop of Hereford 1079–95, under whom the cathedral community established a developing structure of formality. His niche is decorated with the 'ballflower' ornamentation characteristic of early fourteenth-century Herefordshire architecture.

Fernlage was renamed Hereford, but it was probably an ecclesiastical site long before Aethelbert's death.

There is absolutely no doubt that those who lived in England did not get along with those in Wales at that time. The mistrust and animosity was mutual, and was particularly highlighted by King Offa of Mercia (755–94), who built a wall (Offa's Dyke) between Chester and the River Wye specifically to discourage the Welsh from straying over the border into England. It took more than Offa's Dyke to confine Welshmen within the borders of their little country, but those who were caught paid the usual penalty of losing a hand. Today busloads of people from Wales visit Hereford on a daily basis, and have to endure nothing worse than supermarket queues, bad weather and bad manners.

Little is known of the county's first bishop, but evidence suggests that he was appointed in 801. There is also evidence that the community fairly thrived. Livestock farming provided the mainstay of the economy, much as it does today, of course, with milk, butter, cheese, meat, hides, wool and leather products available in abundance. Horses and ponies were highly prized, for they not only provided transport for everyday travel but were most useful in going to war against the Welsh.

Robert de Bethune, bishop of Hereford 1131–48. This dimly lit effigy is situated in the cathedral, and serves as a fine example of early local sculpture.

Robert de Melun, bishop of Hereford 1163–7.

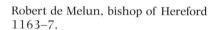

Robert Foliot, bishop of Hereford 1174–86. The wooden crosier is almost certainly a nineteenth-century replacement for the original, which was probably eaten by woodworm.

Between 950 and 1100 a number of churches were constructed, mostly by manorial lords. Like so many other areas of Britain, Herefordshire produced great craftsmen whose skill in working stone and timber has rarely been surpassed. By the time Domesday Book appeared in 1086 Herefordshire had forty churches staffed by clergy who, incidentally, didn't practise celibacy.

Domesday reveals the county as a system of feudal tenures with a social hierarchy, trade system and even architecture bearing similarities to those in Normandy. Typically, village folk were headed by a Norman knight at the top of the social pecking order, whose farming activities provided revenues for a local bishop. The knight – a man of arms – employed 'administrative' officials and estate workers including several stockmen, domestic maids, smiths, carpenters and other skilled craftsmen. French settlers exerted a cultural and lingual influence, manorial dues were paid in pigs, sheep or cattle – despite the existence of an established mint by 930 – and the Welsh continued as a source of suspicion, regret and battle.

The walled city of Hereford was spread over roughly 25 acres, and prior to 1066 there were 103 families living both inside and outside the perimeter wall. Everyday activities were focused on the cathedral and castle, but after the city boundary was extended to the north a new marketplace paved the way for outlets operated by butchers, fishmongers, drapers and leather crafters. Interestingly, the layout of the city was carefully planned and remains the same in essence today.

However, for those living in either the city or the countryside, the constant threat of attack from the Welsh, who at one juncture plundered the cathedral, became a daily pain in the neck. Things came to something of a head on 16 September 1400 when a group of men from north-eastern Wales assembled at Glyndyfrdwy, Merionethshire. Led by the proclaimed Prince of Wales, Owain Glyn Dwr, the group of several hundred – Glyn Dwr's family, friends and devout followers – set out to attack Ruthin and other towns under English rule in the north-east of the province. Their campaign against the English wore on for years, Glyn Dwr enjoying a mixed bag of fortunes, but eventually fizzled out as more and more of his followers lost interest. By 1414 it was all over and although Edward 1 could claim to have made a 'conquest' of the country, he, his men and history cannot correctly claim that the Welsh were wholly conquered, or pacified, for they never have been.

However, with the 'conquest' of Wales the importance of Hereford castle declined, and those who manned it were made largely redundant. Many exchanged their weapons for useful tools and became weavers, dyers, tailors, bakers and millers.

While hitherto the people of Herefordshire had lived largely in ignorance of Wales, her people, geography and geology, trade with the principality in bread and cloth suddenly became an important source of wealth to the city. As prosperity continued the cathedral became more and more grand, but the spread of bubonic plague in 1348 and 1361 made a serious impact on the population.

Rum Chaps

During the medieval period the shire's most famous family were arguably the Mortimers, who originated in Mortemer, near Rouen. Among the greatest of the Marcher barons, the Mortimers 'ruled' for 400 years, roughly from the time of Domesday. Their principal role, along with other Marcher barons including the Clares, Bohuns and Marshalls, lay in stirring up trouble with the Welsh. Whatever lands the Mortimers could conquer was theirs by royal authority; it was very much in their interest, therefore, to provoke the

Welsh as often as possible. Such was the power of this family that they ruled over lands not directly under the control of the king, and for a time they controlled and directed English affairs from Wigmore Castle. Several generations of Mortimers spent their days either kicking seven bells out of the Welsh or plotting against the king.

Henry III came in for a particularly rough time from belligerent barons. While Roger Mortimer III was helping Prince Edward in his escape from Hereford Castle, Simon de Montfort mounted an assault against the prince's father. After a bloody battle de Montfort was defeated by the king, who had been largely supported by Mortimer and his men. Mortimer's son Edmund, meanwhile, had been busy baiting the Welsh – his favourite pastime – and having captured one of the Welsh princes, sent his severed head to the king.

Under Edward II the Mortimers gained further power and they openly rebelled against the king and the Despenser family, who harboured aspirations of becoming Marcher lords. By 1321 civil war had broken out – yet again – and the Mortimers, along with Henry III's grandson the Earl of Lancaster, made their feelings about the Despensers known in the clearest terms. Roger Mortimer IV and his chum the Earl of Hereford captured London, much to Edward II's annoyance, but Mortimer's attempt to overthrow the government landed him a spell in the Tower of London.

With alcohol donated by the bishop of Hereford, Mortimer bribed his guards and escaped to France, and just to add salt to the wounds, he formed an adulterous relationship with Isabella, Edward II's queen. In 1327 he began plotting to invade England. He and his men landed on Britain's east coast and headed for Hereford, which Mortimer used as a base. The king had fled into Wales and was eventually caught, along with Hugh Despenser, at Neath. Despenser's ambitions for social elevation were immediately cut short by a rope, which Mortimer ordered to be tied around his neck, and the king was deposed. To ensure that Edward's monarchic future was ended, Mortimer came up with the usual contemporary solution – he murdered him!

Roger Mortimer – a rum chap by any standards – naturally inclined to taking the throne himself, but Edward III had other ideas. Mortimer was arrested and, for the second time in his life, was banged up in the Tower of London. None of his friends in Hereford seemed the least bit bothered on this occasion, and Roger Mortimer, the most infamous member of this notorious family, was charged with murder and hanged, drawn and quartered.

Evidence in Art

Herefordshire's ecclesiastical buildings provide great insight into the county's medieval life. Records, books and documents – particularly the cathedral's chain-library – are in many instances especially well preserved, but the many works of art are an equally valid source for archaeologists and students of history. Statues and effigies commissioned by the well heeled and executed with the greatest skill have survived, often against the odds. Carved stone effigies of well-known bishops and other dignitaries in the cathedral, for example, have noses and hands missing, but for the most part the survivors are in good condition and tell their own stories.

Vanity, pride and posterity all played their part in the minds of the people who employed sculptors and artists to make such pieces. Sculptures of people would eventually give way to the art of the portrait painter, which in turn would be superseded by portrait photography.

Early sculptures and brasses tell of the wealth of the subjects, their social stature and the types of clothing worn in this cold part of Britain. Knights are depicted in brasses wearing suits of armour, while cloaks, headdresses, necklaces and long flowing dresses

In similar style to the other stone effigies in the cathedral, this is William de Vere, bishop of the shire between 1186 and 1198.

provided contemporary haute-couture for the womenfolk. As in the rest of Britain and Europe before the Renaissance, people are illustrated in drawings in two dimensions – as flat figures on flat surfaces. Three-dimensional art had been reserved for relief work in wood and traditional sculptures. Why man had spent thousands of years drawing in 2D, and only came to appreciate the qualities of depth, perspective and light and shade roughly from Leonardo da Vinci onwards, is a largely unanswered question for masters of the history of this subject, and despite the wealth of this material in Herefordshire, the county is unlikely to offer a concrete solution.

Burnt Out

In the years leading up to the end of the fourteenth century the character of Herefordshire and her people had been formally shaped; a distinct identity had been acquired, which in some respects would remain intact for many hundreds of years. For the majority of folk daily life was physically demanding, tough and tedious.

In the years ahead there would be continuing battles with the Welsh, of course, the bloody battle of Mortimer's Cross between the Houses of York and Lancaster, more bouts of bubonic plague and the usual bleak, cold winters, and while the industrial revolution would transform life in much of the British Isles, Herefordshire would survive 'unscathed' by progress.

The quite magnificent door of Kilpeck church, which includes many figures, is from the Hereford School of Sculpture and dates from around 1140. The first evidence of a church on this site – mentioned in the *Book of Llandaff* – dates from 650. The eighty-five corbels, monster heads and people depicted on the door, and elsewhere, have been subjects of conjecture for many years.

It has been suggested that the two figures on the left-hand side of the arch surrounding the south door at Kilpeck are Welsh warriors because the upper one has a sword and the lower has a lance. The unusual features, however, are the clothes; both have quilted tops and are wearing trousers, neither of which featured in English art until the Victorian era.

A splendidly preserved carving inside Kilpeck church of a rather miserable looking chap – possibly a cleric, who appears to be facing the prospect of a dull day's writing, dipping a quill pen into an ink bottle.

Figures of beasts and a man above the south door of Kilpeck church, symbolism with meaning that has largely been lost. The exaggeration of Biblical morality appears to be a warning to Kilpeck worshippers of divine retribution for transgressors. The people of this small village today are more concerned about speed cameras, spiralling council rates and crime.

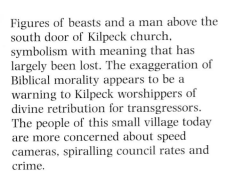

One of the most grotesque medieval symbols to be found at Kilpeck, and at around thirty other churches in England, the sheela-na-gig's true meaning is also the subject of conflicting conjectures. Possibly a fertility symbol, or a warning against lust and avarice, the sheela-na-gig is a naked female with her genitalia most prominently on display. Many in Ireland were destroyed in the seventeenth century because bishops objected to their potential for aiding sexual 'corruption'. Today such images are exploited for this very reason by entrepreneurial pornographers as a fairly fast route to Ferrari ownership.

Dating from the early twelfth century, the font at Eardisley church portrays the same style of stone carving as that found at Kilpeck, Canon Frome and Shobdon Arches. Two armed men are shown, possibly fighting each other. Recent research indicates that the scene might represent a duel between Ralph Baskerville, Lord of the Manor of Eardisley, and Lord Drogo of Clifford who fell out over a land dispute. Baskerville killed Drogo, asked the Pope for pardon, and ended his life as a monk in Gloucester.

Shobdon Arches, the remains of a twelfth-century building carved with figures, grotesques, animals and motifs – a very weathered example of the Hereford School of Sculpture. An acknowledged masterpiece, the figure sculptures have been badly eroded.

Little has been done to protect the finest examples of our native art at Shobdon. These images, from the twelfth century, are beyond saving, but re-creation and restoration are not beyond the ken of the many talented sculptors currently working in the county.

Tympanum with Christ in Majesty at Shobdon Arches. The same style of carving exists in Spanish and French churches, and serves to illustrate the remarkable spread of Christianity throughout Europe. In Herefordshire Christianity naturally came into conflict with Celtic paganism. In recent times creeds and beliefs common to paganism have found favour with 'New Age' travellers, pockets of whom continue to challenge traditional ways of life and senses of decorum around the county.

Garway church also has ancient examples of the grotesque, this figure representing a cross between an animal and a man.

Figures either side of the window at Garway church are well-preserved examples of early representational figure sculpture.

An unflattering sculpture of St Peter above the main entrance to St Peter's Church, Bromyard. This beautiful building also has many features of the Hereford School of Sculpture and is among the county's most historic treasures.

Leominster Priory, where two heads have been carved on either side of the window frames. Curiously, both have avoided providing target practice for bands of marauding yobs down the centuries.

The familiar figure of Christ carved in stone above the west door of Hereford Cathedral. As in the rest of Britain, the influence of the established Church has declined sharply in Herefordshire. Congregations are few and far between, the county's churches now largely serving as historical curiosities.

A bishop in need of a hand is among the many splendid carvings on the west front of Hereford Cathedral.

A chap in dire need of a face wash among the stone carvings on Hereford Cathedral. Representational carving of such detail was far from unknown before the Renaissance, but many modern sculptors have deposited such notions of art in a vast reliquary.

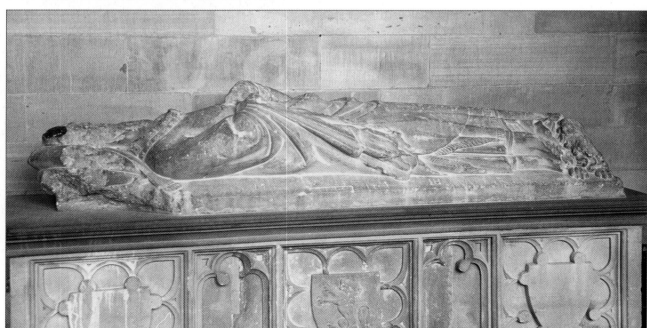

An effigy in the cathedral of Lewis Charlton, bishop of Hereford 1361–9. The poor chap has the facial appearance of having endured several rounds in the ring with Frank Bruno, but is otherwise unscathed.

This magnificent stained-glass window at Eaton Bishop's church dates from 1330 and depicts Bishop Walter, who was given Eaton Bishop by William I.

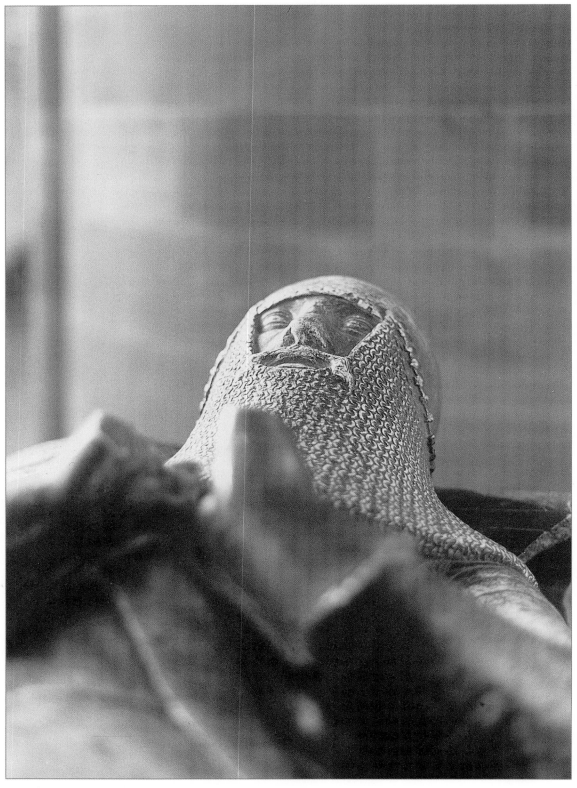

A really superb piece of carving in Hereford Cathedral of Sir Richard Pembridge, who died in 1375. A Knight of the Garter, he fought at the battles of Crecy in 1346 and Poitiers in 1356.

2

A Clean & Pleasant Land, 1400–1850

Philanthropist Lady Margaret Hawkins founded Kington Grammar School in 1632 on profits made by her husband Sir John from the slave trade. The original school building, to which this impression is attached, is currently being restored.

Between 1400 and 1850 the county's wealth increased considerably. Large monastic communities, largely dependent upon agriculture, at first thrived but later went into decline, large country houses and grand, timber-framed buildings were constructed and a greater number of people acquired the skill of literacy. That so many of the great buildings still stand is testament to the manner in which they were designed and built.

Socially, the community was polarised. Wealth was very much concentrated in the hands of the few – a landed gentry – and although large numbers of everyday folk were engaged in occupations that today are reasonably lucrative, the majority got by on comparatively little. Politically, conservatism and support for royalty prevailed, and there were comparatively few 'republican' dissenters, even during the reign of Charles I. Religious denominations comprised the Anglican Church, Quakers, Baptists, Presbyterians and Catholics.

In Leominster the wool trade flourished, although farmers voiced discontent when cheaper fleeces from Spain were imported, and during the sixteenth century Ledbury's cloth and leather industry prospered, only to go into decline during the eighteenth century because of the expense of road transport.

Bromyard was considerably more sleepy than it is today and failed to develop even with the coming of the railway age; its prosperity was based on the cattle, pig and sheep market, but a brisk trade in cloth sustained life for many. During the sixteenth century the town had nearly fifty shops, and in essence it hasn't changed to this day.

The ancient town of Ross-on-Wye was similarly slow to develop. However, one of its most famous sons, John Kyrle (1637–1742), had a profound effect in that he restored much of the fourteenth-century church, brought a permanent water supply to the town and built a causeway to the bridge at Wilton. The town's stone wall, much of which still stands today, was not constructed until the early nineteenth century. By this time Ross's natural defences – the River Wye and its lofty situation – which had once given a degree of protection against disgruntled Welshfolk had become less important.

Kington achieved a degree of fame through the Vaughan family of Hergest Court, where Lady Charlotte Guest found the 'Red Book of Hergest', from which she compiled a book of Welsh mythology – the Mabinogion. The Vaughans were a Welsh family living in Kington which achieved notoriety through its most colourful member – Ellen the 'Terrible'. Disgruntled at the murder of her favourite brother by John Vaughan of Tretower, she dressed in men's clothes and trudged off to Brecon to compete in an archery tournament. Having donned her bow she aimed at the target, turned at the last moment and delivered a high-speed arrow into the man who'd killed her brother. Ellen didn't hang around for long, legged it across several fields and made a successful escape. She later married Black Vaughan who famously returned to Kington as a ghost. Interestingly, this legend continues to form topics of conversation in the town today, and naturally, there are those who claim to have seen the ghost. . . .

Herefordshire's other famous ghosts include Mr Hoskyns of Harewood, near Ross, a particularly mysterious spirit below the bridge at Eardisland, and at Haugh Pool near Yarpole legend insists that there is a lady on a grey horse imprisoned in a goose quill.

A much smaller place than Kington, Weobley witnessed its castle descending into ruin by the sixteenth century, but the village's splendid fourteenth-century church – frequently referred to in jest as 'Weobley Cathedral' – continues to attract droves of tourists from home and abroad. Principally a market town, or village, it boasts a number of fine timber-framed buildings, and although once famous for cloth and weaving, its main 'crust earner' was brewing. Although beer isn't brewed there today, this author can testify, occasionally with regret, that it is still consumed in extremely large quantities.

Left: One of many brasses in the cathedral, this example, of an 'unknown civilian', dates to 1394. Apart from the style of clothing, such figures alone provide little insight into fourteenth-century Herefordshire life. *Right:* A brass of a man in armour, *c.* 1480. At this time English men of arms were employed, by and large, as a warning to marauding Welsh folk.

Centre: A brass of John Stockton, Mayor of Hereford in 1480.

Famous families with Weobley connections included Cornewalls, Tomkyns, Prices, Birches and Foleys, who all slugged it out for political supremacy during the seventeenth century. Their electoral success or defeat was largely based on bribes or threats in varying quantities, but Weobley's influence had declined sharply by the beginning of the nineteenth century. Several businesses closed their doors for lack of passing trade and never reopened. Today Weobley thrives on tourism; during the summer months the village buzzes with folk who spend hours gawping in wonder at age-old buildings which Herefordians tend to take for granted.

Top Drawer

The majority of Herefordshire's monuments were erected to wealthy land owners – well-known figures, many of whom, incidentally, were burdened with what today is referred to as a 'weight problem'. Meat, of course, played a much more prominent role in people's diet than it does nowadays (for those rich enough to afford it), and few subscribed to the modern view that a prize should be donated to 'slimmer of the year'.

At Much Marcle there is the tomb of first Earl of March Roger Mortimer's daughter Blanche, who wed Sir Peter Grandison. Much Marcle became globally famous in the 1990s as the one-time home of serial killer Fred West and, as motor racing enthusiasts are aware, the current Earl of March plays a more useful role than his ancestors by organising important race meetings at the family seat, Goodwood House, every year. Incidentally, the Earl of March's younger sister, Lady Louisa, lives at Presteigne to this day – just a few miles from the Mortimers' original seat.

Sir John and Lady Kyrle are also represented in effigy form at Much Marcle, while an effigy of John Scudamore exists at Kentchurch. The Scudamore name lives on in the popular Hereford school, Lord Scudamore, in Friar Street.

In Kington, the Lady Hawkins' secondary school takes its name from the woman married to Sir John Hawkins. She founded the school in the early seventeenth century on profits from her husband's grubby dealings in the slave trade. Regrettably, the oldest part of the school is no longer used for its original purpose and is currently being restored.

In collaboration with the Church and monarchs, established families wielded great power from great houses inhabited by generations of their successors over centuries, but the Industrial Revolution resulted in a shift of power. New captains of industry who had

Evidence of great wealth in Pembridge church. Local historian Blount, writing in 1675, attributes these effigies to the Gours, Lords of Marston, near Pembridge. The rear pair of figures are a civilian and a woman from the early fourteenth century, while the other pair – from later in the same century – are a priest in a cassock and a woman wearing a mourning dress, possibly Lord Gour's wife.

made fortunes, principally in manufacturing, rather than inheriting them, gradually began to replace established aristocracy.

Croft Castle had been inhabited by generations of the same family, but the Shropshire-based Knight family, who had amassed a fortune in the iron industry during the eighteenth century, took over. John Arkwright, grandson of Lancastrian Sir Richard who invented the spinning-frame, bought Hampton Court, near Dinmore, one of the country's oldest and most beautiful houses. Arkwright made sweeping changes to the building during the 1830s, and in more recent times a large sum has been spent on restoration work.

Bits and pieces

When the Russians and Americans began to explore space in the 1960s it was discovered that the Great Wall of China was the only man-made object that could be seen on Earth from the confines of a spacecraft. By the 1990s the New York landfill site had been added to this list – a reflection on vast consumerism in some quarters of western society. The disposal of rubbish and waste has in recent times become a problem, and sensible solutions are few and far between.

In Herefordshire the increasing popularity of car boot sales serves as just one illustration of a consumer society in which discarded objects – mostly junk and white elephants – are offered, often at extremely low prices, to bargain hunters. As a society we have become 'purchasers' and after using our material acquisitions to the full for their intended purpose, or becoming bored with them, we either discard them or pass them on to someone else.

In most Herefordshire households today there are televisions, videos, CD players, one or more cars, cameras, personal computers, clocks, watches, an abundance of clothing and footwear, telephones, washing machines, fridges and personal ephemera such as photograph albums. Simple annual sales figures of books show that everyday folk are reading less than in Charles Dickens's day, the attraction of the Internet having resulted in many erecting fewer and fewer book cases in their houses. Electric lighting, heating, instant energy for cooking and clean water are all, of course, taken for granted. A temporary cut in the electricity supply is viewed as a gross inconvenience for domestic users, and can lead to serious financial loss and disruption for industry and business.

It is impossible to know exactly what Herefordshire folk living more then 150 years ago would have made of late-night viewing on television, for example, or of children conducting meaningless conversations on mobile phones as they troop off to school to cough through their first cigarette of the day, or of sitting stationary in a traffic queue when walking is so obviously quicker and healthier. It's possible only to guess at the answers to such interesting questions. However, there is ample documentary evidence that the ordinary folk of yesteryear had very few possessions, and those they did have were treasured for their practical, sentimental and aesthetic value.

Naturally, the large houses of the county were extremely well furnished, many having extensive libraries, particularly as the nineteenth century advanced. Curtains, bed linen, family paintings, cutlery, crockery and clothing were all present in large quantities, but a very different picture emerges of poorer people. A minority had little more than the clothes in which they stood, or lay, while others might have had simple possessions such as candlesticks, thimbles, minimal bedding and crockery. More prosperous folk kept a few animals – hens for eggs and a pig or two for home consumption – but gloves, hats and a second pair of boots or shoes were, by and large, luxuries. Incidentally, fat from animals also provided fuel for candles.

Worn clothing was repaired, food never discarded, discipline maintained, and beer and cider were staple lubrication at meal times. Tobacco smoking, which began in Britain roughly 500 years ago, was slow to catch on in the county, principally because the infamous weed was originally very expensive and, therefore, exclusively within reach of the rich, but as prices came down more and more men and women took up the habit. At first tobacco was smoked in pipes, usually of clay, and as many keen gardeners today are aware, it's almost impossible to dig over a tract of soil, especially in city gardens, without finding fragments of these fragile objects. Cigarettes would arrive in large quantities towards the end of the nineteenth century, and were even viewed by the government as a daily necessity by the outbreak of the First World War in 1914.

As time progressed men, particularly in the countryside, acquired guns as an effective means of supplementing the contents of the larder. Whether poached or shot legally, there was rarely a shortage of game in Herefordshire, and this remains the case today.

Between the Hedgerows

By the beginning of the nineteenth century Herefordshire's population had reached 88,438 (1801 census figure). The major towns of Ross, Bromyard, Ledbury and Leominster each had upwards of 5,000 inhabitants, and as economic progress continued, there became greater diversity in employment opportunities. Alongside the agricultural workers, millers, corn merchants, cattle dealers and bakers there were doctors (still relatively rare in 1850) and vets, and by the 1830s a second branch of the legal profession – solicitors – had been established. More schools and houses were built and although poverty existed for many, social improvements were being made across the board.

The established church continued to play an important role in the lives of most folk – Church of England vicars were among the highest paid members of society – but Catholics, Methodists and Baptists provided an alternative for 'dissenters'.

For the majority, transport was by Shanks's pony, with the result that shoe-makers continued happily in business, but the coming of the railways would lead to greater geographical mobility and the creation of jobs and new occupations.

From the mid-nineteenth century onwards the face of Herefordshire would begin to change. Women would slowly gain a degree of independence, initially thanks to the invention of the typewriter, and although agriculture continued as the county's most important economic activity, a migration of folk from the countryside to the city was an inevitable outcome of the establishment of industry and commerce.

This fifteenth-century tomb at Kington church of Thomas Vaughan, slain at Banbury in 1469 with his wife Ellen the Terrible. Ellen was quite something: disguised as a man she attended an archery contest, shot her brother's murderer through the heart with an arrow, and made a successful escape. People who commit such crimes today aren't normally commemorated so lavishly.

A large and most impressive mural of Christ on the wall of the church at Michaelchurch. A fifteenth- or sixteenth-century impression, it is now faded, though discernible, and drawn with badly proportioned arms and hands. The picture of Christ is surrounded by everyday tools and weapons – both were necessities for basic survival in this border counties village 500 years ago.

The tomb in Hereford
Cathedral of Richard Mayor,
bishop of Hereford 1504–16.

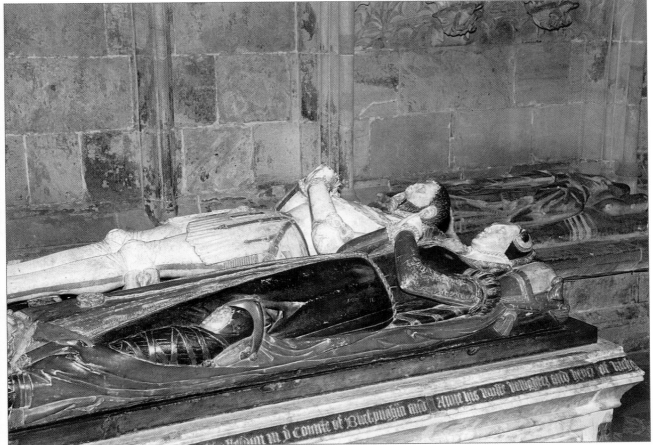

The colourful and highly detailed tomb in the cathedral commemorating Alex Denton and his first wife Anne Wilson, who died in childbirth in 1566. The baby lies to the left of Anne's leg. Denton died in 1576 and was buried in Buckinghamshire with his second wife. This magnificent tomb was restored in 1975.

Not a 1970s pop star but John, first Viscount Scudamore (1601–71) of Holme Lacy. His enduring legacy was the promotion of the Redstreak cider apple.

George Coke, bishop of Hereford in the mid-seventeenth century. The effigy, in Hereford Cathedral, is original, while the elaborate canopy was erected by his descendants in 1875.

Bishop Theophilus Field, former chaplain to Charles I, shown in traditional preaching pose. This image was restored by his descendants, Thomas and Mildred Shumaker, in 1986.

The monument to Colonel John Birch in Weobley church. A Lancastrian by birth, Birch became MP for Leominster, his military prowess also earning him the governorship of Bridgwater, Bath and Bristol under Oliver Cromwell. An inscription describes him as 'vindicating the laws and liberties of his county in war, and promoting its welfare and prosperity in peace'.

Philanthropist John Kyrle (1637–1724) provided a water supply for the town of Ross-on-Wye. This relief portrait hangs on Kyrle's house in Ross. After he died the building became an inn – the King's Arms – but was converted into three shops in the early nineteenth century.

1690

John Kyrle - 1637 - 1724 - was a local benefactor. His generosity was immortalised by the poet, Alexander Pope, who referred to him as 'the Man of Ross'. He laid out the Prospect for the townspeople and provided a water supply.

He was a great planter of trees. Here he is shown, as an eyewitness described him, in his plain brown suit setting off on one of his tree-planting expeditions. His spade is over his shoulder and he carries a bottle of liquor. He was accompanied by two or three workmen, depending on the sort of work he was doing.

The large house on the right was the Kyrle town house with a large garden behind. After his death it became an inn, the King's Arms. An entrance was cut through the centre of the building, and the garden was made into a bowling green.

At the beginning of the nineteenth century the inn was closed and the building was divided into three shops.

The facade is reconstructed from architectural and pictorial evidence.

A stainless steel placard in the centre of Ross depicts John Kyrle setting off in his plain brown suit on one of his many tree-planting expeditions, accompanied by a man with a barrow laden with trees. Kyrle's life was immortalised by Alexander Pope, who referred to him as 'the Man of Ross'.

Portraits of John Kyrle hanging on the front wall of the Man of Ross pub in the town centre.

Market day in Ross, 1776. Sheep are driven past The Swan and Falcon Inn (left) to the market in St Mary's Street. Map-maker Isaac Taylor is illustrated with his wife and children leaving their house (right) to complete his survey of Gloucester.

1776

The scene is set on a market day. Sheep are being driven into town to be sold in Broad Street and a reluctant cow is urged towards the Beast Market in St. Mary's Street. The Swan and Falcon Inn on the left did a busy trade on these occasions

In the eighteenth century this end of High Street was much higher than the present street. Three feet of soil was shovelled away in 1833 to bring the surface to the level of the new Wilton Road, which was cut into the hillside. The houses on the extreme right of the picture were demolished to build the road.

Before this road was built the only access from the river was by Dock Pitch - now Wye Street - a steep and muddy track which carried all the traffic from the east. High pavements saved the pedestrians from the worst of the mud. The original doorway for no. 53/4 High Street can be seen at first floor level on the facade. Even with the high pavements it must have been reached by steps

Isaac Taylor, the map maker and engraver, lived in this house, with his wife and children. Here he is shown taking his leave of his wife and daughters before starting out to complete his survey of Gloucestershire, which was published the following year. His assistant carries his hodometer for measuring distances.

Above: Horatio Nelson 'woz 'ere'. The plate attached to the wall of The Swan and Falcon Inn at Ross commemorates the great admiral's visit.

Right: John, Lord Viscount Bateman, who owned Shobdon, and at whose behest the three Shobdon Arches were preserved and re-erected in his park. This relief of Bateman can be seen on the wall of Shobdon's church.

One of two similar and charmingly hideous grotesque carvings in wood above the doors of the Farmers' Club in Hereford's Widemarsh Street. Such ugliness is symbolic today of the agricultural community's anger towards the erosion of a way of a life essentially unchanged in centuries. Blame is cast upon the prime minister, of course, but the problems facing country folk go well beyond politics.

Below: Herefordshire is, of course, famous for cider. This political cartoon from 1761 illustrates the 'Jack Boot' being hanged – the Jack Boot being a pun on Scottish prime minister Lord Bate who imposed taxes on many goods, including cider.

The ROASTED EXCISEMAN

3

Towards War, 1850–1918

Three farmers sharing a joke at Bromyard market, or are their smiles induced by camera shyness? Thick tweed jackets were worn by farmers and farm workers all year round; Herefordshire is not among Britain's warmer or drier counties.

The arrival of the railways in Herefordshire in 1854 created engineers, mechanics and generations of small boys who dreamt of becoming an engine driver. Steam engines were also used for pumping Hereford's water supply around the city, but the first motor cars would not be seen in the county until the beginning of the twentieth century, when bicycles were also making impact on the lives of everyday folk.

While the village streets were caked with mud during wet weather, pavements and hard-surfaced roads were built in the city. Market days were great social occasions, and that which is known as organic farming today was still known as farming. Pests and weeds that threatened crops were dealt with by labourers who worked tirelessly for little reward.

During this period a small number of individuals made such impact that their legacies are still considered to be important today. Born in 1855 in Widemarsh Street (at what is now the Imperial Inn today), Alfred Watkins became famous as a photographic innovator and for his theory of ley lines. He was also a brewer, archaeologist and miller. Watkins's

One of Herefordshire's most famous sons, Alfred Watkins, pictured here on the front cover of Ron Shoesmith's excellent book *Alfred Watkins: A Herefordshire Man* (Logaston Press). Watkins, a pioneering photographer who invented an advanced type of light meter, also wrote his theory about the possible existence of ley lines. These are, according to Watkins, ancient tracks that guided people from one place to another – often religious sites – in straight lines. *Right*: The Imperial Inn in Hereford's Widemarsh Street where Alfred Watkins was born. For many years this building – of minor historical importance – has been used as a restaurant.

daughter once described him as a 'rough diamond to look at' – a broad-shouldered, bearded chap who wore Harris Tweed irrespective of the weather. His coat, which had no fewer than fourteen pockets, was constantly filled with tools and papers, and occasionally became too heavy to lift easily. A keen swimmer and rower, he once canoed the Hereford to Gloucester canal – parts of which are still intact. Watkins's interest in photography led to the production of several new gadgets. Based at his father's flour mill in Friar Street, Hereford – the building was used for a variety of successful manufacturing operations in the late twentieth century by Bob Marriage – Alfred Watkins produced his actinometer from 1890. This measured light intensity by automatically counting the time taken for sensitised photographic paper to darken. He then went on to make an exposure meter, marketed as the Bee Meter – to maintain the impression of something efficient and small – a darkroom clock and his factorial calculator which helped in the difficult craft of attaining the perfect development time for a photograph. Watkins's exposure meter was especially successful, with no fewer than 1,400 being sold at a guinea apiece (£1.10) in the first year of production.

In September 1921 Watkins presented a paper he'd written – *The Old Straight Track* – to the local Woolhope Society. He argued that all trackways followed straight lines marked out on a sighting system, thus laying the footings for his theory of ley lines. Just five months after reading his paper to the Woolhope Society, he went on to publish a book – *Early British Trackways* – but this interesting tome would become equally famous for Buckridge, the craftsman who bound each copy. Buckridge had something of a grievance against his wife and her foster-mother, and took the extreme measure of solving his problem by murdering both of them.

A Drink from the Soil

Although Herefordshire was once among the primary hop-growing regions of Britain – hops were first planted in the county in 1724 – this industry had declined significantly by the 1970s. Cider production, on the other hand, has risen inexorably. Of the main producers – Symonds, Westons and Bulmers – Bulmers are by far the most important and, of course, the world's biggest. Now with outlets in many countries throughout the globe, H.P. Bulmer is also among Herefordshire's leading employers and apple growers.

Interestingly, the business was started because its founder, H.P. Bulmer, was virtually unemployable. The old boy suffered very badly from asthma and wasn't expected to live a long, healthy life. As a result he didn't receive a conventional education and was forced largely to fend for himself. The son of a vicar, the Revd Charles Henry Bulmer, he was fortunate in having sufficient funds to begin a business on his own account. His mother advised that food and drink were probably his best bet on the grounds that neither ever went out of fashion, and she had something of a point.

In 1887 (Queen Victoria's Golden Jubilee) H.P. Bulmer began making cider at Credenhill – close to where the SAS is based today – and called upon the services of the family pony, Tommy, to operate the mill. During 1888 premises were established in both Maylord Street and Ryeland Street – the factory at the latter site was sadly demolished in 2002 to make way for a housing estate – and in the autumn of the same year the small concern produced 4,000 gallons of cider. With a dearth of local cider apples – pears were plentiful – fruit was imported from Somerset, but this situation would change down many years. Today it's difficult to travel for more than a few miles in any direction without spotting orchards of apple trees.

Much of the cider-making process remained unchanged for the best part of 100 years, and when Bertie Bulmer mooted the idea of creating a cider museum during the 1970s, a number of the company's employees pithily remarked that there was no need, as they had spent many years working in one.

Today this thriving company has many varied interests in the drinks industry and continues to expand its worldwide activities. Incidentally, many local people refer to Hereford cider as 'Gloucester Lager'; it might be coincidence that one of Bulmer's best known brands is 'GL'.

A Modern Hereford

From the 1850s onwards Hereford's infrastructure began to change. The city not only expanded as the population rose, but the types of shops and businesses founded were not significantly different in essence from those of today. Both the railway and Hereford–Gloucester Canal brought more folk from Wales and Gloucestershire into Herefordshire, many of whom took up residence. Although the first railway line, between Hereford and Shrewsbury, opened in 1853, more were added piecemeal in the years that followed. The Hereford to Worcester line, for example, opened in 1861, and as a link was also established to South Wales coal became an important part of everyday economic life. Regrettably, many of the lines linking the smaller towns and villages have long since disappeared; their revival would inevitably be welcomed by those whose lot is to sit in long traffic queues twice a day.

In the second half of the nineteenth century Hereford businesses included banks, drapers, shoe shops, grocers and even a music shop. By the 1880s the Green Dragon Hotel had become a popular haunt. It has survived a mixed bag of fortunes over the years and prosperity has recently returned, despite its being clad by large tracts of ugly scaffolding during 2002.

The local courts were kept extremely busy, not only in dealing with civil litigants but, human nature being what it always has been, with miscreants whose crimes in some cases make today's villains appear tame and unimaginative. The use of a sturdy gatepost as a weapon by an aggrieved farm worker was among several similar cases reported by the *Hereford Times* during this period. Theft of livestock from farms was not uncommon, whereas today Herefordshire farmers are more likely to be robbed of valuable machinery.

Horses for Courses

In 1886 Karl Benz was correctly credited with having designed and built the world's first motor car, a crude three-wheeled device that paved the way for the twentieth century's most important man-made tool. By the beginning of the twentieth century a number of companies had been founded throughout Europe to build cars and capitalise on this new invention. Motor vehicles were necessarily expensive to buy and run, and became the exclusive property of the well-heeled.

In Herefordshire cars were relatively few and far between, and reactionaries who put their trust in horses hated the new-fangled devices. A small number of serious accidents added fuel to the fire of their mistrust. For pioneer motorists local roads were unmade and rough, and few ever completed a journey without incurring punctures. Despite early difficulties, though, it was obvious that cars offered the opportunity for travel, speed, freedom and excitement. By 1904 the Midland Automobile Club had started running competitive events at the Shelsley Walsh hillclimb venue in Worcestershire, and apart

The road through the centre of the small village of Peterchurch in the Golden Valley – visited by C.S. Lewis in the 1950s – is just as narrow today, and almost as peaceful. In the nineteenth century the people pictured would have been predominantly engaged in agriculture in some way or other. Contrary to popular belief, many women were engaged in full-time employment.

from interruptions by two world wars it has been doing so ever since. Many thousands of people from both Herefordshire and Worcestershire flocked to Shelsley Walsh to watch cars and motor bikes thundering up the hill, the majority arriving on foot having walked many miles. Motor cycles were also developed and became popular; being much cheaper to buy than cars, they appealed to a much wider audience.

Despite the obvious advantages of motorised transport there were serious drawbacks, other than the usual toll in injuries and fatalities. By 1914 much of Europe was at war, and although horses continued as the staple transport of armies, motor vehicles, including aircraft, opened up greater opportunities to military strategists. Men could be taken to battle zones in greater numbers and more quickly than ever before, and the result was a heavy death toll.

More than 2,000 men from Herefordshire – nearly 400 from the city alone – lost their lives in one of the most senseless and prolonged wars in human history. The Herefordshire Regiment – later renamed the Herefordshire Light Infantry – fought with great bravery and distinction in both world wars, but the county's most distinguished military men – originally named the Long Range Desert Group – came into being during the Second World War as the Special Air Service.

Churches all over the shire have tabulated lists of men who died serving their country during the wars, St Martin's in Hereford having a particular affinity with the SAS, who are known locally as 'The Regiment' or 'Regiment blokes'.

A late nineteenth-century scene at the Ledbury Market Hall, where trade is carried on in much the same manner today. Motorised transport has taken the place of horses, and noise pollution has increased dramatically, but at least shoppers no longer have to negotiate large dollops while crossing the road.

Despite the loss of men aged between sixteen and fifty from the county in the First World War, the population continued to rise. By 1921 it was officially quoted at 113,189, more than 20,000 up on the 1801 census figure.

Immediately before the outbreak of the First World War rising numbers of women were being engaged in paid employment, but whereas previously their lot had been in menial jobs – domestic service and trade – office work requiring literacy and numeracy skills became increasingly important.

Quietly By

During the First World War Herefordshire remained much the same as it had always been. Agriculture predominated; H.P. Bulmer continued its successful cider-making operation, providing invaluable employment for locals. Men who were sufficiently lucky to return home after hostilities in Europe did so to ponder on the complex reasons for their survival.

Psychiatric help for those suffering from 'shell-shock', or post-traumatic stress disorder as it's known in modern 'psycho-babble', was practically non-existent. Like the majority of British mental hospitals, St Mary's at Burghill – a grand shrine to Victoriana – had progressed little in the field of psychiatric medicine.

Few imagined that human conflict would occur on such a terrible scale again but, of course, it did.

Richard Dawes, dean of Hereford 1850–67, was an educational reformer in whose time Scott's restoration of the cathedral went a long way towards preventing serious deterioration. This magnificent effigy in the cathedral is in Carrara marble by sculptor Matthew Noble, and the chest is of alabaster and marble by Brindley and Richards.

The small village of Eardisley, near Kington, during the early part of the twentieth century. Small girls pose dutifully for a photograph on the main road. Architecturally this scene has changed very little while the outlook for small girls of this age has changed dramatically. Today's kids would not risk talking to each other while standing in the middle of the road; lorries, cars and mobile phones have put paid to that.

The nineteenth-century road from Bromyard to Stourport with a toll house in a landscape that hasn't essentially changed. The two young children, possibly the tollhouse keeper's, would have seen many travellers every day but benefited little financially from the takings.

A lonely, bleak picture of an unidentified boy at a Bromyard toll gate, and a typically unimaginative, but technically interesting, example of early photography. Ironically, charging money for travelling by vehicle into town centres could become a reality once again as traffic congestion increases on a daily basis.

The Square in Bromyard; locals are setting up stalls in the hope of brisk trading, *c.* 1900. The buildings are the same today, while the roadway has become a busy car park. I sat on a bench here in the spring of 2000 with top car designer Andrew Dyson discussing the downfall of Britain's motor industry, and we concluded that, rather like Bromyard, it never changed with the times.

Opposite: Canon C.S. Palmer, rector of Eardisley 1866–1906, and his wife. This nicely preserved photograph hangs in Eardisley church; modern colour photographs will not fare so well as the colours tend to fade in time.

A fine portrait of Henry Morgan, bachelor of law, who was vicar of Stoke Lacy between 1871 and 1887.

Master of Arts, Henry Morgan, took over Stoke Lacy church as vicar from his father, and remained at the helm until 1937. Their descendants went on to found and successfully run the Morgan car company in Malvern, Worcestershire.

Morgan three-wheeled cars are commemorated in stained glass at Stoke Lacy church.

Bicycles from the early part of the twentieth century, designed without a horizontal crossbar to protect the modesty of the fairer sex. Two gents and a woman, who seem to have lost a sixpence and found a halfpenny, don't appear to be too keen on a long cycle ride.

Also a keen cyclist, Sir Edward Elgar (right) is commemorated, along with other famous composers, in stained glass at Bromyard's church. Elgar could never be considered among 'top-flight' composers, but his Cello Concerto, made famous by Jacqueline du Pré, stands the toughest scrutiny on merit.

PURCELL · SAINT CEADMON · ELGAR

Retired dentist and author of several books about Herefordshire, Derek Foxton has a passion for early bicycles and motorcycles. He is pictured with his Sunbeam, which was once the property of Sir Edward Elgar. Considered as the Rolls-Royce of bicycles during the early part of the twentieth century, it was made to the highest attainable engineering standards, but stands as a monument to two-wheeled discomfort.

Herefordshire was once famous as a major hop-growing county but this useful crop – used almost exclusively in beer brewing – has declined in importance since the 1970s. As this picture in the Bromyard Heritage Centre shows, hops once provided seasonal employment for hundreds.

Dressed in clothing more appropriate for a ballroom, hop workers harvest the valuable crop in the hop yards before transporting them to the oast houses for drying. Hands behind his back, the man in the centre appears to be the farmer, ever wary of getting value for money out of his hard-working staff.

Stoke Edith railway station, 1908. Hop pickers are returning home with their belongings and bunches of hops. The picture is interesting for students of period costume – ladies of this era played tennis in similar attire!

Many families from the county, the Midlands and south Wales looked upon the hop harvest as an annual holiday – a chance to escape, meet other people and share in the great camaraderie that exists to this day. Holiday or not . . .

. . . there was no getting away from hard work.

Heady work among ripe, aromatic hops prior to bagging. Stern concentration and relentless physical effort burnt off a fat-rich diet of wholesome farm produce. The response of these people to suggestions of half a grapefruit for breakfast, a stick of celery for lunch and a bowl of clear carrot soup for supper would be interesting – and most predictable.

A remarkable example of a 'professional' photograph in which the lensman has sought, and successfully captured, three farm workers in a natural 'pose'. This wasn't easy to attain with cumbersome cameras requiring a comparatively long exposure. The image has also survived extremely well.

Avenbury Court hop yard, 1905. Social convention
dictated in favour of gentlemen wearing collars and
ties, and ladies donning full-length gowns. It was
improper for the latter to display as much as an ankle
in the days before the feminist movement burnt its
collective bra.

Dried hops are poured into a hop pocket, directed into
position by the feet of the seated man with a little help
from gravity.

After being bagged the hops are transported to a brewery, where they are used for flavouring beer. A local farm worker kindly made a hop pillow for this author. Its aromatic properties are thought by some to give restful sleep. In reality the stench is so pungent that sleep would come more easily on a pillow of baked cow dung.

The lonely life of a farm cook at harvest time. She was kept busy providing meals for dozens of people, but was always kept away from buildings in which crops were stored for fear of fire from the stove causing disaster.

Great social change, particularly in education from the 1960s onwards, probably means that the descendants of these hop workers are well-travelled, educated professionals working in skilled jobs. Whether the latter are any happier, though, provides interesting subject matter for sociological research.

Whatever happened to British manufacturing industry? Here is photographic evidence that it once existed. Ex-chairman of ICI, Sir John Harvey-Jones, who is also a Herefordshire resident, argues emphatically that Margaret Thatcher and her policies were responsible for the wholesale destruction of indigenous manufacturing.

An early twentieth-century photograph at the premises of Hall of Madley, a picture that might have been used to illustrate characters from a Thomas Hardy novel. The bearded man with the bowler hat and winged collar – apparently taking notes – is distinguished socially from 'the men' by possession of a pencil and the ability to use it.

Above, left: A model in Bromyard's fascinating Heritage Centre depicting a hop worker with a pole. This simple implement is used for guiding miles of string up which the bines grow; this traditional method is still used today (*above*). Modern technology has singularly failed to replace a wooden pole and a bag of string. *Left*: This work is deceptively hard requiring physical fitness and strength. Novices complain that their neck, arms and back ache, while old hands love the work.

Political correctness is of no value, concern or interest on Herefordshire farms, where the division of labour between male and female has been stringently defined for decades. Women's work is women's work, and it would be an extremely brave man who argued otherwise.

Harvesting hops with a tractor and trailer instead of the horse and cart of yesteryear. For students of social history, Herefordshire farms are places where life hasn't changed much in 200 years or more. Workers use the same vocabulary and speak in the same dialect as their forebears – and work just as hard despite mechanisation.

Unloading hops for drying today – a tedious job for young and old alike, but at least it's a job. The exodus from country to city has created imbalance and is probably unsustainable.

'Ship be in the meadow, cows be on the 'ill, all I ever eats is 'tatoes, no wunder I be ill.' Sheep at auction have been an inescapable feature of Herefordshire's economy for centuries, apart from dire outbreaks of Foot and Mouth Disease in 1967 and 2001. Smartly dressed gents eye up wool and mutton bargains.

Opposite, top: 876 prime beef cattle on sale at Ralph Knight's auction in Bromyard's Smithfield Market, 17 October 1901.

Ploughing the soil away from the hops in spring. The tractor driver is so obviously an authentic Herefordian countryman. His cap is tilted in traditional fashion to one side of his head. Incidentally, tractors from this period were so well made that hundreds regularly appear at agricultural shows and make for endless conversations among tractor anoraks.

A tradition unlikely to die; a group of chaps enjoying the fruit of the annual hop harvest – relaxing with pints of Herefordshire-brewed ale. It is also cause for celebration that small, independent breweries continue to flourish in the county and provide welcome alternatives to cider.

The interior of a general store in Bromyard, where four members of staff await customers between the wars. As much a meeting place for conversation as anything else, such shops still exist throughout the county, but the big supermarkets have made them increasingly unattractive as a business proposition.

Road making the hard way, with hand tools, manpower of all ages, and a powerful steam tractor. Steam tractors are great attractions at the Bromyard Gala and Marcle Steam Fair today, and the roads of the county are just as rough as ever.

Construction of Herefordshire's railway network began roughly in the mid-nineteenth century. The efforts of thousands of men in creating such a huge feat of engineering would be thwarted in the mid-twentieth century by short-sighted political engineering.

The railways came to Bromyard in the mid-nineteenth century, and not only allowed local folk to travel into Wales and as far afield as London, but also enabled hop producers to import harvest labour from Birmingham and the Black Country. Agricultural goods of all kinds were transported to markets more quickly, whereas nowadays large trucks add to road congestion, costs and environmental pollution.

Construction of a road bridge over the railway; work continues while the photographer presses the shutter button. Just one worker has been unable to resist looking at the lens, such was his natural curiosity about the radical new technology.

Despite the hundreds of people who used Herefordshire railways on a daily basis, the rails linking many towns and villages had been ripped up by the 1960s. The Leominster to Bromyard section was closed on 15 September 1952, and that from Bromyard to Worcester last ran in 1964. In 2002 the county needs an efficient rail network more desperately than ever . . . but it won't get one.

Hereford Rowing Club in about 1890 with a much more attractive club house than the wholly undistinguished 'box' that suffices for today's members.

C.W. Radcliffe-Cooke MP from Much Marcle. He was known as the Member of Parliament for cider because he promoted the drink so well.

A painting in the Hereford Cider Museum depicting a couple of farm workers enjoying an alcoholic break during harvest. Cider has played an important part in the local economy for decades, and this remains the case today. Cutting crops by hand and stacking into sheaves had largely died out by the 1950s when combine harvesters gradually began to replace mechanical binders. Tea and coffee would also replace traditional refreshments of cider and beer at meal times.

Henry Percival Bulmer (1867–1919), founder of what would become the world's largest and most important cider makers. The son of a vicar, he was advised by his mother to go into either the food or drinks industry on the grounds that the human need for both would never go out of fashion. Asthma prevented him from receiving a university education, and he set up shop in 1887. He became the company's first chairman in 1918.

The Revd Charles Henry Bulmer, father of Henry Percival Bulmer who founded Bulmers Cider. Charles was rector of Credenhill from 1861 to 1910.

Edward Frederick Bulmer (1865–1941) joined his brother H.P. Bulmer as a partner in the cider company in 1889, and succeeded him as chairman in 1919, a position he held until his death.

'She mounts again and rages more, than ever vixen did before.' It is not thought to be politically correct to use a ducking stool to punish errant women today, but this ancient practice is occasionally resurrected in the county to raise money for charity.

Members of the Hereford Regiment pictured at Ross-on-Wye shortly after the First World War. The majority bear an uncanny resemblance to Captain Blackadder.

A grand statue near the Priory Church commemorates those from Leominster who died between 1914 and 1918 in the First World War. Nearly a century later the world is still at war!

4
The Age of Reason, 1918–2002

Despite attempts by government departments and other institutions to create obedient,
automated, standard human beings with a BBC voice, sickly complexion and the ability to
contribute handsomely to HM Treasury, colourful characters still exist in Herefordshire.
This old warrior, snapped necessarily in haste at the Three Counties Show, has enjoyed his pipe
for many decades, and has no intention of risking his health by giving it up.

As the 1920s unfolded it became inevitable that the motor car was not going to go away, as some had predicted. Herbert Austin's diminutive Austin 7 didn't quite bring motoring to the masses, but it certainly went a long way towards providing basic motorised transport for those able to stretch to an asking price of around £100. Herefordshire's roads were of a type better suited to tractors, but these wonders of modern agriculture weren't in general use in the county until the mid- to late 1940s.

Horses were used for general farm duties and a ploughman's lunch comprised a bottle of cold tea, bread and an onion, which added little to dispel the widely held view abroad that Britain had the least imaginative cuisine. For the purpose of growing fresh vegetables and maintaining marital harmony, allotments were popular among the county's menfolk who, in the comfort of a shed, could imbibe, smoke and chat with like-minded souls without incurring the wrath of the hard-working little woman at home. The landlords of the county's pubs would gain handsomely as a result of the decreasing popularity of allotments in the latter half of the twentieth century.

Post-war social policy from central government dictated that the city and the principal market towns would change, most visibly for the purpose of housing the growing working population. In the 1950s the City Council began large building programmes at Newton Farm, Moor Farm, Whitecross and on land close to the Technical College. Intended as affordable rented accommodation, the houses were built to last for sixty years, but such was the quality of materials used in their construction, the majority are expected to last considerably longer.

Along with H.P. Bulmer Ltd, Wiggin Alloys in Holmer Road became one of the county's principal employers, the latter becoming responsible for manufacturing, among other things, blank coins.

Up until the 1970s, however, cultural activity was confined within a narrow social group. It was largely centred around the Three Choirs Festival, and periodic organ recitals in the cathedral. Largely thanks to the efforts of local artist Peter Manders, jazz was heavily promoted, with a number of venues attracting some of the world's best known figures, including Billy Butterfield and Humphrey Lyttleton, but successive attempts to convince Herefordians of the benefits of theatre failed dismally until the 1990s.

Cinemas and discos generally prospered, and there is little doubt that the local economy is greatly benefited by the presence of the SAS, whose once favourite watering holes – the Booth Hall and Grapes Tavern – were traditionally full of 'squaddies' at weekends. As Herefordians of the older generation readily recall, Peter MacLeese was among the most infamous members of the local regiment – a great soldier and a hard fighting man, with a colourful character and a turbulent life that has passed into legend.

The SAS breeds many heroes, of course, but the accolades bestowed upon individuals for acts of bravery in theatres of war are not publicly recorded, and such is the mutual respect between the local community and the SAS that confidences are always respected.

The Good and Great, Bad and Ugly

Seduced by the charmingly rural nature of the county, a number of well-known artists from various disciplines have lived, or continue to live, in Herefordshire. Although originally from the Forest of Dean, playwright Dennis Potter lived and worked for many years in Ross-on-Wye. His last television interview, with Melvyn Bragg, was conducted with bravery and courage, for the great man was dying of cancer and relied on a potent cocktail of morphine and alcohol to deaden pain. The *Sun* newspaper recorded his death with the headline: 'Dirty Den's Dead'. . . .

Poet Laureate John Betjeman and novelist Bruce Chatwin were also well acquainted with the county, the latter's book *On the Black Hill* being set in the foothills of the Black Mountains.

In the art world Walenty Pytel has become internationally famous for his metal sculptures, principally of animals and birds. Like so many artists, Walenty struggled hard for many years to get his work recognised, and there were times when it would have been fairly easy to have thrown in the towel and looked for a 'proper job'. On several occasions many years ago he was forced to fish in the River Wye merely in order to feed his family, but things are very different today, his work selling in some instances for healthily high sums. Similarly, David Eatwell, who grew up in the city, spent much of his adult life

Internationally renowned and acclaimed sculptor Walenty Pytel claims that he was once so poor that he had to fish the River Wye in order to feed his family. Famous for his welded animals in metal, Walenty's work is in global demand, but many examples can be studied on public display throughout Herefordshire.

painting pictures that no-one wanted to buy. Thanks to dogged persistence, innate talent and help from the Internet, his work is now highly regarded around the world.

A number of famous and talented musicians, apart from Sir Edward Elgar, also have close links with the county including record producer Matt Butler, who was born in Herefordshire. Having completed his 'apprenticeship' under Sir George Martin, Matt has worked closely with Sir Paul McCartney, Mick Jagger, Gordon Lightfoot and Steve Harley to mention but a few luminaries from the rock world, and continues to produce and promote new bands from studios in Hampton Bishop.

In the early 1970s rock legend Mike Oldfield came to live on Bradnor Hill above Kington, and produced his first album, *Hergest Ridge*, named after another hill also above Kington. Oldfield went on to record *Tubular Bells*, one of the most successful pieces of the twentieth century. Published on the Virgin record label, this album launched Sir Richard Branson's colourful career. Incidentally, during the 1970s Mike Oldfield played in a quartet at Penrhos Court, Kington, an eating and drinking establishment with its own brewery in which Monty Python star Terry Jones had interests.

Ian Hunter of Mott the Hoople, sundry members of the Pretenders, Robert Plant of Led Zeppelin and Roger Whittaker among others all settled in the shire at one time and another, but such is the ephemeral nature of 'pop' that many have long since been forgotten – except in Herefordshire.

One man who will never be forgotten is the infamous Fred West who, along with his wife Rosemary, was among Britain's most deranged serial killers. Fred, from Marcle, was, by his own inference, responsible for many more deaths than those with which he was charged, but cheated justice in a Birmingham prison by his own hand before being brought to trial. In all probability his wife will remain incarcerated until the day she dies for crimes which almost beggar belief.

Serious crime is extremely rare in Herefordshire, unlike much of the United Kingdom, although murder, conspiracy to murder, sexual assault and arson are not unknown. And whereas the Bobby on the beat some thirty and more years ago was prepared, and expected, to give sparring yobs a good hiding, today's boys in blue tend to mediate, caution and live in constant despair of bureaucracy, budgets and BS.

In the field of motor sport, the county boasts of many heroes and characters, and even has a Formula 1 team – Minardi based in Ledbury, a far cry from the technologically primitive industries of past centuries in this sleepy little town. Just as incongruous is Hereford's current bishop, the Right Revd John Oliver, who, affectionately known as 'Bish the Bike', owns an extremely powerful motorcycle, and uses it for its intended purpose with great enthusiasm and relish. The first 'non-family' chairman of H.P. Bulmer, Peter Prior, is also a great fan of powerful motorcycles. After his time with the cider giant Peter went on to produce a report about motorway cafés, denouncing them as expensive and mediocre. Happily, his report brought change for the better.

Veteran racing driver Barrie 'Whizzo' Williams from Bromyard continues to be a regular competitor in British circuit racing, having successfully 'sparred' with all the great Grand Prix names of yesteryear. Leominster, on the other hand, will always be associated with the late Bill Bengry who, among his many accolades, won the International RAC Rally Championship in both 1960 and 1961. Bill, who, strangely, was made an honorary maharaja, became the only man in history to win a gold medal three times in the now defunct Liège Rally. Bengry went on to works drives for both Rover and Peugeot, and as if

Leominster garage proprietor and international rally driver Bill Bengry won the International RAC Rally Championship in both 1960 and 1961 in a Volkswagen Beetle, which his granddaughter Jackie Partridge still drives. One of the county's great characters, Bill had a reputation as an eccentric workaholic, but in reality he was a man who was interested in all things right until the end.

to confirm his reputation for eccentricity, entered a Rolls-Royce Silver Shadow for the 1970 London to Mexico World Cup Rally. While charging through Portugal, part of the Rolls's rear suspension broke on the left-hand side. Being a practical, resourceful chap, Bengry repaired it with part of a gatepost and continued to Mexico. Upon return to England he advised Rolls-Royce to design its cars with a gatepost on both sides of the rear suspension on the grounds that, in Bill's words, 'it was a better arrangement than the "effing" rubbish that you lot designed.'

Just a few miles up the road from Leominster, the village of Shobdon was once home to two of the 'greats' of motor racing. Both Peter Walker and Innes Ireland farmed there, their motor racing careers running parallel with business duties. Peter Walker, who among other things won the 1951 Le Mans 24 Hours in a C-Type Jaguar, was a popular character at the Horse and Groom, Hereford, for many years, an accident at Le Mans in the mid-1950s having ended his driving career. Sadly, Peter died in a house fire in 1984 at the age of seventy-five, but his son Tim still lives in Shobdon.

Innes Ireland had a chequered career in both sports cars and Formula 1, but top stardom in the fickle world of Grand Prix eluded him. Ireland's place in Colin Chapman's

Bill Bengry was one of the few people to use a Rolls-Royce in international rallying. He is pictured taking part in the 1970 London-to-Mexico event. The Rolls broke its rear suspension in Portugal, which Bill successfully fixed with part of a gatepost. Upon return to Britain he advised Rolls-Royce that it should fit all its cars with gateposts on the grounds that 'it was a better arrangement than the "effing" rubbish that you lot designed.'

Lotus outfit was taken in the early 1960s by Scottish genius Jim Clark, and Innes lost out. Bob Evans, who once ran business interests in Ledbury, also drove for Lotus – a once truly great Grand Prix outfit that, sadly, no longer competes.

Beyond all these good folk, however, the county's greatest motoring-cum-aviation character was Hamish Moffatt, once dubbed by the national newspapers as the 'Bosbury Biggles'. Hamish hit the headlines in the mid-1990s after an 'incident' at the Verzons Hotel, near Ledbury. The Vintage Sports Car Club meets at this venue annually on New Year's Day, and for many years Moffatt's 'party piece' was to fly over in his Gypsy Moth aeroplane and bomb the hotel with bags of coloured flour. However, on one occasion his spectacular trick didn't go exactly to plan. A strong wind led to one or two flour bags being blown off course and a local resident, disgruntled that the contents of her washing line had suddenly changed colour, phoned the police. A serving RAF helicopter pilot present at the car meeting also reported Hamish to the Civil Aviation Authority for flying at an unlawful height. Needless to say, Hamish was hauled before the local beaks and the CAA, both bodies taking exception to his hilarious activities, and fined. In his customary manner, Hamish paid his dues without complaint – 'the boy done wrong' – but voiced the bitterest of dissent as to the size of the fees he handed over to his lawyers for defending him.

And finally on the motoring theme, John Day from Moreton-on-Lugg achieved global fame during the 1970s as a sponsor of Grand Prix cars. His company, John Day Model Cars, pioneered new techniques of casting model racing cars and became hugely successful. Many other manufacturers in this field followed Day's example, and today he is universally cited as the 'Father of the model car world'. John, now in his seventies, continues to make models of cars and commercial vehicles, but prides himself most on possession of what is undoubtedly the filthiest and fullest car ashtray on the planet!

Herefordshire Today

Writing in the *Hereford Times* in 2001, a man from Gloucester claimed that he'd always considered his home town as the dullest place on earth . . . until he'd visited Hereford. It is, however, difficult to define and categorise cities as dull. Hereford, like any other place, would be enlivened by the presence of a few hundred naked people dancing in High Town, but such an unlikely scenario would not be long-lived.

In reality the county breathes roughly in economic tune with the rest of the planet; it has to for survival. Industrial estates generally thrive, with a huge variety of businesses specialising in extremely diverse activities. On the outskirts of the village of Madley, Marconi's satellite communications systems are state-of-the-art – the 'listening' dishes a feat of engineering and at night a work of art in themselves.

Farming has declined in some respects, and 'diversity' has become one of the most used words in the countryside. Farmers and landowners are facing up to the challenges of today's countryside problems in the same way that so many are attempting to address the social problems that so obviously afflict the city.

At one time during the 1990s many reckoned that Hereford was Europe's fastest-expanding city. New housing developments spread like a rash and, as homes were heavily in demand, property prices went through the roof.

In the future, the people of the county will have no option but to face up to stark facts of road congestion.

Agricultural shows have been a feature of local life for centuries and give opportunities for all kinds of traditional activities. A fly-fishing contest at Homend Park, Stretton Grandison, is captured here during the warm summer of 1990.

Several times a day the city is grid-locked by traffic and angry motorists, frustrated by their lack of progress over badly maintained roads.

Herefordshire has changed in so many ways during the past twenty years or so, but the basic tenets remain. Farmers moan and groan, as they have for centuries, local people blame the prime minister for all their ills, the pubs continue to serve experts who know the answer to everything and the River Wye flows monotonously from the mountains of mid Wales – as it always has. Some things will never change.

A rare derailment near Kington station in the 1920s became a topic of conversation among locals for months. The smartly dressed gentlemen – all wearing caps – appear to be momentarily more concerned with recording their role in the proceedings for posterity, which is understandable at a time when the majority of everyday folk did not own a camera.

'I never saw such a mess in all my born days.' The Old Radnor Company, whose trucks were derailed at Kington, didn't think a lot of it either. In May 2002 seven people lost their lives when a train was derailed at Potters Bar. In the aftermath many armchair experts gave their views as to methods that might be devised to ensure that rail tragedies never recur. Here is photographic evidence that rail accidents have been inevitable since the invention of *The Rocket*. Incidentally, no railway now runs through Kington.

Broad Street, Bromyard, 1930s. A small market 'satellite' town, where life has not changed fundamentally in decades, this scene could easily be recreated today. The same buildings are intact, and people go about their daily business in much the same way. The modern counterpart of the policeman on the far right of the picture would, confronted with a similar situation today, jump into the middle of the road to prevent the car with its headlamps facing the camera from making further progress. Broad Street is one-way today and the car would be travelling against prevailing traffic.

Broad Street, Ross-on-Wye, in either the late 1920s or the 1930s, with a Bullnose Morris (foreground) and an Austin 7 behind it. Although traffic volume has increased dramatically, this scene remains much the same today. A busy town with a proliferation of good pubs, interesting shops and an annual music festival, Ross is a good example of a civilised British community that thrives in an increasingly competitive world.

Cider making at Bulmer's in the 1930s. The apples were brought in from orchards by horse and cart prior to being crushed. The same principle is used today except that apples are brought in by motorised transport. For most Herefordians the strong smell of apple juice that has wafted across the city for generations during September and October is the first true sign of autumn.

Collecting apples for Bulmer's cider, a labour-intensive job at a time of virtually full employment in Herefordshire before the Second World War. Interestingly, two of the men in this picture are wearing ties.

A team of coopers hard at work making cider barrels for H.P. Bulmer. This ancient and highly skilled craft is now largely, but not wholly, forgotten as wooden casks have given way to more modern materials such as plastic and stainless steel.

A fine illustration in the Hereford Cider Museum of cider production at Bulmer's. The large press on the right squeezes juice from the apples, leaving a residue of pomace. Originally thought of as a 'waste' product, it was discovered that pomace could be made into pectin, which is used to set jam. The site in Ryelands Street on which the Bulmer's pectin department was built is now a housing estate.

Traditional cider making involved a great deal of hard physical effort, but the result was always worth it. Small, independent cider makers, such as Suzie and Ivor Dunkerton's company near Pembridge, continue to produce traditional ciders and are a great asset to the county.

Opposite: While the majority of orchard workers in this picture are happy to pose for a photograph the man in the middle foreground appears to be expressing indifference to, or disapproval of, photography by carrying out the pre-war equivalent of 'mooning'. 'I don't hold with them new-fangled gadgets.'

Founder of the Hereford Cider Museum, Bertram Bulmer.
Something of a character, 'Bertie' once shot a duck that
fell on the opposite side of the river bank from where he
and his young dog Paddy were standing. In order to teach
Paddy the art of retrieving, Bertie removed his clothes,
and swam with the dog across the Wye. After locating the
duck Bertie put it in his mouth and muttered to Paddy:
'This is what you have to do – just like this'.

Before the advent of powerful four-wheel drive tractors and ingenious agricultural implements to harvest crops in little more than a couple of days, this same activity took several weeks. By comparison, the old methods were inefficient, but the sheer numbers of people required to work on the land held closely knit communities together. For most of the year traditional craft activities and labouring have disappeared, and despite moves towards organic farming, they will probably never return.

Opposite: Farm workers drinking cider from a traditional cask encased in a wicker basket. Free of additives and sugar, the cider was still and dry, and would not appeal to modern-day cider devotees accustomed to sweet, 'gassy' products. Trousers with missing buttons are a practical aid to the effects of excessive imbibing.

WIS
DE
CARTHY
MORGAN
BRAY
ALE
PERRETT
IPS
RICE
TCHARD
NIE

L. Cpl LEONARD
Mne FREDERICK W
A.B. CYRIL J. SKIN
P.O. EDWARD SMITH
L/Sea CHARLES C.
Pte THOMAS A. TA
Sgt WATKIN L.T.
War Corrpdt WIL
F. Sgt WILLIAM G.
Cpl HARRY WOODY

The people of Ledbury remember those who died in the Second World War with a monument in the High Street depicting an airman, an Avro Lancaster and Spitfire fighter aircraft. The picture is illustrated on tiling while a mosaic is used for the sailor (*left*).

A 1950s Hereford United squad specially selected for a benefit match. The photograph was kindly provided by ex-Leicester City, Shrewsbury Town and Hereford United player Ralph Oliver who, understandably, couldn't recall the names of all the players. However, as far as he could remember they are: back row, left to right: Ray Daniel (Welsh international), Jack Kelsey ex-Arsenal (third from left), Ralph Oliver, Roy Chapman and ex-Swansea and Cardiff player Gilbert Beech. In the centre of the front row is Tommy Hughes, ex-Wales, and second from right is England international Tommy Lawton.

Hereford United in the early 1960s when players received a tenner a week, the game was one of skill and attack, and the Edgar Street ground was richly supported by local fans. The team's ascent to the Second Division in the 1970s was followed by a period of decline. Today Hereford United – which was formed in 1924 – is in crisis and struggling to survive.

Welsh international and Hereford United great Ray Daniel receives treatment for a back injury from trainer Albert Bradley, late 1950s.

A successful Hereford United squad from the early 1960s. Back row, left to right: Roly Morris, Peter Isaac (keeper), Ralph Oliver, Don Bennet, Ray Daniel and Tony Jacques. Front row: Ian McKintosh, Tony Biggs (ex-Arsenal), Bobby Dixon, Archie Styles and Gordon Nutt.

One of the county's fittest 84-year-olds, Tommy Best, the 'Old Man' as he is affectionately known, played football for Hereford United, Cardiff City and many foreign clubs before retiring from the game in the 1950s. A born comedian, with a natural ability to entertain, it is widely believed that he should have been selected to play for Wales, his national team. A victim of racial prejudice, Tom bears no grudges, but occasionally reflects on what might have been. No one who knows Tom is likely to forget him.

Estate agent Andrew Morris is also chairman of Westfields FC, a body that continues to help youngsters realise their ambitions as budding Beckhams.

John Day from Moreton-on-Lugg, whose successful company John Day Model cars pioneered new techniques in the field of die-cast miniatures. He sponsored Formula 1 aces Hans-Joachim Stuck and Ronnie Peterson during their spell at March during the mid-1970s. John is still in the same business today, and believes in all Christian virtues except retirement.

Mick Wildig (left) was among Hereford's unique characters. He kept himself extremely fit, and competed in running marathons and sponsored walks well into his seventies. A Bass drinker and regular visitor to the once famous 'back bar' at the Green Dragon Hotel, Mick is fondly remembered for his interesting stories, while some try to forget his singing. At the age of seventy-nine, Mick was approached by two yobs while wheeling his bicycle along a Hereford street late at night. Without motive the yobs attempted to beat him up; happily, they both came off second best.

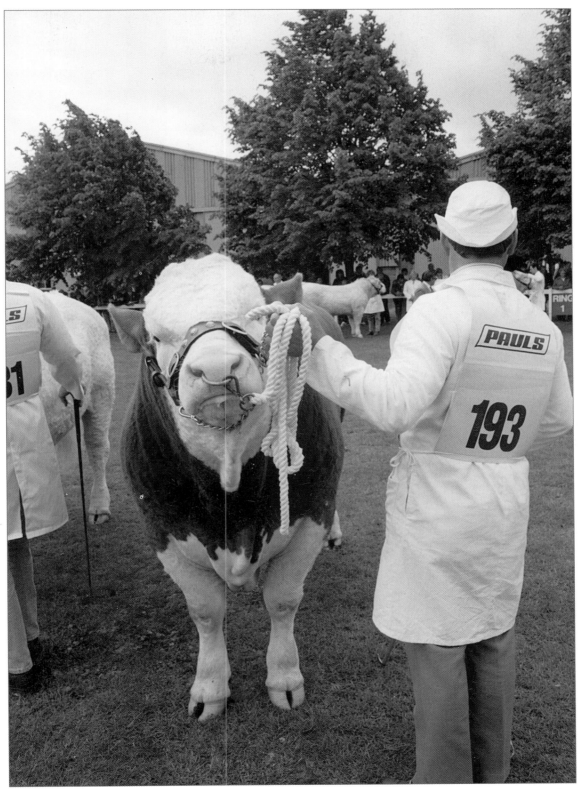

Not a Herefordshire person but a Hereford bull, a great symbol of the county's agricultural heritage that has become an icon of local enterprise recognised the world over.

Delightful statues above the Michael Oxenham art gallery in Bromyard, depicting a painter and nude model, possibly the nearest Herefordshire has publicly come towards recognising the permissive society.

Painter David Eatwell struggled hard for years to gain recognition in the art world. Largely thanks to the Internet he has been able to bring his talents to the attention of the global market. David paints in Britain, Greece and Germany in a style of his own. A huge talent from Hereford, Eatwell's name and work are assured an important place in the history of art.

Originally from Shropshire, local artist Peter Manders is internationally renowned for his landscapes and cariacatures. He contributes to a wide variety of publications and through his interest in jazz has met and illustrated the majority of legendary musicians of the twentieth century in this field.

Many a happy couple will remember the man who recorded their wedding day on film. Richard Hammonds has been among the county's leading photographers for nigh on fifty years. Semi-retired and living in Marden, Richard will be remembered for his wit, irreverent humour and ability on the end of a camera shutter button.

Below: For many years Barrie Griffiths held the post of chief photographer at the *Hereford Times*. Although an all-rounder, he will be best remembered for capturing some of the best, and worst, days of Hereford United's fortunes.

Hilda and Mike Tasker from Ashperton, near Ledbury, who in the mid-1990s planted an arboretum in their back garden to commemorate Mike's parents. Around 2,000 trees, including exotic rarities from as far away as the Himalayas, are represented. Mike and Hilda have arranged a plot in their unique garden where they are to be buried.

Endearing eccentric Major Ted Widgery is an archetypal gent with the hoarding nature of a squirrel and tendency to live in a bygone age. This author once spent six hours in Ted's garden making a bonfire from heaps of past copies of the *Daily Telegraph*. The inferno burned for two days. Sufficient copies remain to run a power station for about a week.

Ex-chairman of H.P. Bulmer Ltd, Peter Prior CBE, with his wife Prinia astride one of their large motorcycles. A great leader and successful industrialist, Peter Prior turned Bulmers into a hugely profitable company, and is among Britain's most respected business talents. He served with the Intelligence Corps during the Second World War and was awarded the Croix-de-Guerre in 1944. However, one of his proudest possessions is a 1941 charge sheet for 'unsoldierly behaviour'; he was caught with his hands in his pockets! The framed charge sheet hangs on a wall at home next to his CBE. In 1981 he wrote himself into the *Guinness Book of Records* for the highest parachute jump by a civilian – 27,000ft. Among his many great achievements he has chaired several Royal Commissions, and today in his mid-eighties remains as active and affable as ever. It is not possible to delve into all of Peter's achievements and successes, but it suffices to record that he is held in the very highest regard. *Below*: Prinia and Peter Prior, he in full uniform as the deputy lord lieutenant of the county.

Richard Cookson, owner of Britain's only barometer shop. Based in Leominster, Richard and his staff specialise in barometers, clocks and watches, repairing instruments from all over the world.

Wolfgang Zeuner from Yarkhill achieved worldwide fame when he sought to prove the Hannibal legends by walking a herd of elephants over the Alps. Assisted by England cricketer Ian Botham, Zeuner discovered that elephants have an extraordinary ability to climb hills, which is more than his Bugatti did at Vintage Sports Car Club events on occasion.

Colin Jones, alias 'Boxer', enjoyed something of a reputation as a biking tearaway as a younger man. Despite advancing years he is never likely to be tempted by the comfort and warmth of a motor car in place of his beloved trike. This Reliant-engined homebuilt special is, apparently, ideal for trips to Sainsbury's coffee shop.

Maz Haig is a familiar sight in Hereford's High Town, where she regularly sells copies of the *Big Issue*, a publication devoted to helping homeless people.

In constant search of complete freedom, Dale Horton has been on the road for the past ten years in a horse-drawn wagon he made himself. He chooses to live in the wagon alone, and makes a living by building interesting furniture. Many of his pieces are made from woven brambles and saplings.

In a caring compassionate Britain there will always be room for unfortunate people. Barry Ridley will be known to many hundreds of shoppers as the man who occasionally asks passers-by for the 'price of a cup of tea'. Mentally incapacitated through no fault of his own, he is not to be denied.

Mark Cole displaying evidence that society's view of social workers as wearers of open-toed sandals at the wheel of a Citroën 2CV is an unhelpful stereotype. The large bruise on his bicep was the result of being bitten by a young teenage girl during the course of his duties.

Below: One of the county's many long-term unemployed, Chris Still (53) taught chemistry at a university for twenty-two years. After redundancy he took up a post teaching building at Hereford's Technical College before government cutbacks forced him out of work and on to the dole. Like so many in his position Chris, from Bartestree, is multi-talented in both the sciences and arts. His plight is surely a symbol of a society that has yet to challenge seriously the foolish tragedy of scrapping able people on the grounds of age.

A delightful and charming young lady from Mansell Lacy, Andrea Hughes has a most unusual job as a teacher of Tai Chi. This ancient Chinese practice, derived from the martial arts, has a growing number of devotees in Britain, many of whom adopt the discipline's philosophical teachings as an alternative to traditional British ways of life.

Motoring enthusiast Carole Felton from Ross-on-Wye is among the few lucky ladies to drive exotic sports cars regularly. She is pictured here with her Ferrari Testa Rossa.

Traffic cop Nigel Phillips has served as a policeman in the county for more than twenty-five years. He's one of those people for whom nothing is ever too much trouble, a pillar of the community pictured fixing a neighbour's lawn mower.

More than 90 per cent of the charcoal used on British barbecues is imported from abroad. A small, but significant, amount was manufactured in the traditional way in Herefordshire during the 1990s. British summers, typified by appalling weather in recent years, quickly dampen enthusiasm for cooking alfresco.

Master mechanic Mike Hibberd from Mordiford is one of the county's most remarkable people, possessing the extraordinary ability to fix almost anything and everything with a piece of wire.

The Three Counties Show, held every year on the showground at Malvern, is a great annual agricultural event for the combined counties of Herefordshire, Worcestershire and Gloucestershire, though Herefordians traditionally eschew association and identification with their near neighbours from the north and south.

Mastercraft Cycles in Hereford's Bridge Street was started by Eddie Thompson (far right) in 1953. Run today by Nigel Quinton (left) and his wife Lynette, this fabulous shop hasn't changed one bit in fifty years, and has remained successful because of this. Eddie once talked me out of buying a new bicycle from the shop on the grounds that there was nothing wrong with my old one. Such honesty is rare, but continues at Mastercraft to this day.

Edward Pritchard, whose family has been in the 'rag trade' for more years than Edward cares to remember. His clothing shop in Hereford's King Street is a model of style and good taste, with a national reputation for service and the best in quality. One of Hereford's treasures.

Peter Brundrett, a local character and proprietor of Hereford's sole remaining tobacco and pipe shop. Although small, which is part of its attraction, Peter's shop is a smoker's delight as it caters for all tastes.

James Heggie, whose father Charles founded his
butcher's shop at Hereford's Whitecross in 1956.
The business continues to flourish under James's
helmsmanship, and has won many awards for its
outstanding homemade produce.

Architectural planner Ron Pritchard is a local
character who, having tired of Hereford's
traffic congestion, swapped his Range Rover for
more efficient forms of transport. A bicycle
suffices for short trips of around 20 miles, and a
microlight serves for long-distance journeys.
A prolific writer of letters of complaint to the
local press on all subjects, Ron is one of God's
own prototypes.

Retired art teacher Mike Christopher has a unique talent for making detailed models from scrap household objects, including cars, trucks and aeroplanes. He is pictured with a fairground wheel – his latest creation. There are many people engaged in this kind of activity, but Mike is particularly remarkable because his vision is seriously impaired.

Originally from Marcle, near Ledbury, serial killer Fred West took his own life in a Birmingham prison while on trial, along with his wife Rosemary, for multiple murder. It is thought that further victims remain unaccounted for. Rosemary West is serving a life sentence and is unlikely to be released. Their house in Cromwell Street, Gloucester, where the remains of victims were discovered, was demolished out of a sense of respect and revulsion. The saga of the Wests is an incomprehensible chapter in human history but, regrettably, they won't be Britain's last mass killers.

Now a member of the House of Lords, Peter Temple-Morris was for many years the MP for Leominster, who became so disenchanted with some aspects of Tory policy under a succession of leaders, from Margaret Thatcher to William Hague, that he walked across the floor of the House. An affable, cheerful, intelligent man, who has worked tirelessly for his constituency, he will be fondly remembered as a modernist, who combined traditional decency with the sense and perspicacity to encourage change.

Graham Paisley (left) and David Lee, leading lights of the local Vintage Sports Car Club, enjoying a pint in the winter sunshine at an old car meeting at the Verzons Hotel near Ledbury.

Not a Herefordian, but a resident of nearby Radnorshire with close connections to Herefordshire, Bill Boddy OBE, pictured at a local vintage car meeting. Doyen of motoring journalists, Boddy, as editor of *Motor Sport*, captivated a world audience for more than half a century with his acerbic wit and authoritative views. Now in his eighties, 'the Bod' is also the author of several superb books on motoring topics.

Roger Collings, brother-in-law of the Duke of Gordon, at the wheel of a 1904 Mercedes 90HP with which he attempted to set a speed record on the Leominster by-pass before it was officially opened.

Garage proprietor Jon Simpson from Weobley with his extremely rare 1968 Jaguar XJ6. This car was one of a handful of pre-production prototypes and was used extensively by journalists at around the time of the production car's public debut. It is one of several historically important vehicles resident in the county.

Top record producer Matt Butler has worked with Sir Paul McCartney, Mick Jagger, Steve Harley, Gordon Lightfoot and other 'greats' of the music world. Matt continues to produce and promote new talent in a global market of fluctuating fortunes. Stiff competition from other technology-led leisure interests has led to a sharp decline in record sales in the pop industry, and the downward spiral appears to be unstoppable.

Making a record in the Chapel Lane studio, Hampton Bishop, is exhausting work, involving long hours of intense concentration. Here, Matt Butler (right) and members of the band Parker (Ian Parker, left, and 'Morg the Org') take a break to listen to a piece they recorded in March 2002 for the BBC. Proceedings are 'supervised' by . . .

. . . Ravi Sharman, a frequent visitor to the Hampton Bishop studio. Like Matt Butler, Ravi has worked with the biggest names in the music industry, but finds the peace of Herefordshire's countryside most compelling.

Gypsy guitarist Angelo Debarre (left) from Paris and violinist Chris Garrick from Perpignan during a break from recording a new album at the Chapel Lane Studio, Hampton Bishop. Both are correctly acknowledged and credited with genius status on their respective instruments.

Lead singer of local band Blush Gary Bexton is among the many talented musicians and performers in the county who gig around Britain for fun, money and the need to practise their art. The car decoration is by Gary's eldest son Seb, aged ten.

Landlord of the Buckingham Inn in Hereford's Whitecross Road, John Wood (right) – 'Pecker' to his friends – who recently bought a fully operational Dennis fire engine because as he pointed out: 'I didn't have one when I was a kid'. John, a mechanic by training, has worked in the pub trade for many years, and is among the great characters of the city. A past mayor of Hereford, Colin Rumsey (left) is well known as a racing cyclist, a sporting activity for which he dons slightly more suitable headgear.

Whereas ponies once provided everyday transport, trekking through the countryside is now a major attraction for people of all ages. Such business ventures also provide farmers with a useful alternative to their more traditional but economically declining activities.

Opposite: Everyday Hereford folk engaged in Christmas shopping, December 2001. High Town hasn't changed architecturally in decades, but the huge growth in population has given everyone just a little less pavement space.

ACKNOWLEDGEMENTS & PICTURE CREDITS

The author is grateful to the following: Bromyard Heritage Centre, Hereford Cider Museum, Ralph Oliver, Peter Prior, Matt Butler, Avril Harrison and Simon Fletcher.

Author Laurence Meredith at Chapel Lane Studio, Hampton Bishop in spring 2002 contemplating life, the universe and the lunch menu at the Bunch of Carrots, of which he cites lunch as the most important. The author of thirty-four books – the vast majority on German classic cars – he claims that cycling along Herefordshire's country lanes is the second best activity in the known universe. The best activity? Smoking his pipe! *(Matt Butler)*